THE REFORMATION
Wʜᴀᴛ ʏᴏᴜ ɴᴇᴇᴅ ᴛᴏ ᴋɴᴏᴡ ᴀɴᴅ ᴡʜʏ

Edited by J E M Cameron

THE REFORMATION
WHAT YOU NEED TO KNOW AND WHY

Michael Reeves & John Stott
Foreword by Lindsay Brown

MONARCH
BOOKS
Oxford, UK & Grand Rapids, USA

Published by Monarch Books
an imprint of
Lion Hudson IP Ltd
Wilkinson House, Jordan Hill Road,
Oxford OX2 8DR, England
Email: monarch@lionhudson.com
www.lionhudson.com/monarch

ISBN 978 0 85721 874 2
e-ISBN 978 0 85721 875 9

First published by Hendrickson Publishers Marketing, LLC, P.O. Box 3473, Peabody, Massachusetts 01961, 3473, USA

Acknowledgments

Part II first appeared under the title *Make the Truth Known: Maintaining the Evangelical Faith Today* (Leicester, UK: Universities and Colleges Christian Fellowship). Delivered in Abergele, Wales, Easter 1982, it formed John Stott's UCCF 1981–1982 Presidential Address. This text, updated in 2016 by kind agreement, is used with permission. Copyright: UCCF.
Appendix 1 first appeared in *In Depth,* a publication of Crosslinks (April 2014). This text, also updated in 2016 by kind agreement, is used with permission. Copyright: Crosslinks
Scriptures taken from the Holy Bible, New International Version®, NIV®. Copyright © 1973, 1978, 1984, 2011 by Biblica, Inc.™ Used by permission of Zondervan. All rights reserved worldwide. www.zondervan.com. The 'NIV' and 'New International Version' are trademarks registered in the United States Patent and Trademark Office by Biblica, Inc.™

A catalogue record for this book is available from the British Library

Printed and bound in the UK, April 2017, LH26

'To those who have been called, who are loved by God the Father and kept by Jesus Christ. . . . I felt I had to write and urge you to contend for the faith that was once for all entrusted to the saints'

Jude, servant—and earthly brother—
of Jesus Christ (v. 3)

'That one sentence did so exhilarate my heart, which had been so wounded with guilt for my sins, that immediately I felt a marvellous comfort and assurance. That Scripture is more pleasant to me than a honeycomb.'

Thomas Bilney, early Cambridge Reformer,
on justification by grace through faith

'The Reformers loved not their lives even unto death, so that *we* could receive the precious and eternal gospel intact. In this age of amnesia, relativism and superficiality, we must hold fast to this same gospel, and pass it on. For we too walk in that triumphant procession of God's prophets and apostles, spurred on by a great cloud of witnesses.

'Cambodian Christians went through their own Neronian persecution, under Pol Pot. They always knew themselves to be a counter-culture, and that to follow Christ would mean being crucified by a sinful world and cruciformed by a holy God.'

Don Cormack, author of *Killing Fields, Living Fields:
An Unfinished Portrait of the Cambodian Church*

Contents

Responses to the Reformation from across the world may be found at *lausanne.org/reformation*

Reformation Timeline

In so modest a volume only the barest story may be contained of the remarkable work of grace which played out in the bravest of lives. Each name below merits a book chapter of its own, as does the life and death of each martyr not included here. The inclusion of several leading figures not appearing elsewhere in this book is to invite readers' further exploration.

In the few instances where dates are unverifiable, we have shown those most commonly used.

1324	John Wycliffe, 'Morning Star of the Reformation,' born in Yorkshire, England
1369	Jan Hus born in Husinec, Bohemia[1]
1384	John Wycliffe dies in Leicestershire, England. His challenge to contemporary beliefs was continued by a diffuse group known as the Wycliffites or (derisively) Lollards.

---

1. Onetime Rector of the University of Prague, himself influenced by Wycliffe, and whose writing would influence Luther.

1407	James Resby declared a 'heretik.' Burned in Perth, Scotland in 1407 or 1408[2]
1412	Jan Hus appeals publicly to Jesus Christ above church authority[3]
1414	Jan Hus lured to Council of Constance. Burned in Constance, Switzerland
1416	Graduands at St Andrews University required to swear resistance to Lollards
1433	Paul Craw (or Pavel Kravar) from Bohemia burned in St Andrews, Scotland
1450	Johannes Gutenberg invents the printing press
1466	Desiderius Erasmus born in Rotterdam, Netherlands
1483	Martin Luther born in Eisleben, Saxony
1484	Huldrych Zwingli born in Wildhaus, Switzerland
1487	Hugh Latimer born in Leicestershire, England
1489	Thomas Cranmer born in Nottinghamshire, England
1491	William Tyndale born in Gloucestershire, England
1494	Martin Bucer born in Sélestat, France
1495	Thomas Bilney born in Norfolk, England

2. See the classic *The Story of the Scottish Reformation* by A M Renwick (Christian Focus Publications).

3. Marked the start of Bohemia's Reformation. Unnamed 'common men' were burned this year, probably the next-earliest martyrs. Over the course of the fifteenth century there was a spiritual dawn in several European countries. To borrow from Reformation scholar Heiko Oberman, the Reformation was the great harvest of the preceding centuries. Martin Luther himself was standing on the shoulders of giants.

1499	Peter Martyr Vermigli born in Florence, Italy, and John a Lasco in Łask, Poland
1500	Nicholas Ridley born in Northumberland, England
1505	Luther joins Augustinian monastery
1504	Heinrich Bullinger born in Aargau, Switzerland
1509	John Calvin born in Noyon, France
1513	John Knox born in Haddington, Scotland
1516	Erasmus publishes Greek New Testament
1517	Luther posts 95 Theses to door of Castle Church, Wittenberg
1521	Diet of Worms. Luther taken into protective custody in Wartburg Castle, where he translates the New Testament into German. Henry VIII publishes his *Defence of the Seven Sacraments* against Luther and is awarded the title 'Defender of the Faith.'
1522	Luther completes German translation of the New Testament
1526	William Tyndale's English New Testament completed
1528	Patrick Hamilton burned for heresy in St Andrews, Scotland
1531	Thomas Bilney burned for heresy in Norwich, England
1532	Thomas Cranmer consecrated as Archbishop of Canterbury
1534	Henry VIII declared 'supreme head of the church in England.' First complete edition of Luther's translation of the Bible.
1536	Calvin arrives in Geneva. First edition of his *Institutes* published. Erasmus dies. William

Tyndale executed. Lady Jane Gray born, probably in Leicestershire, England

1546 Luther dies in Eisleben, Germany

1547 Henry VIII dies. Succeeded by his evangelical son, Edward VI

1549 Book of Common Prayer published

1551 Martin Bucer dies in Cambridge

1553 Death of Edward VI. First cousin Lady Jane Gray crowned as Queen of England, but deposed after nine days.

1553–8 'Bloody' Queen Mary ascends to the throne and restores Roman Catholicism to England

1554 Lady Jane Gray beheaded

1555 Nicholas Ridley and Hugh Latimer burned in Oxford

1556 Thomas Cranmer burned in Oxford

1558 Elizabeth I succeeds Mary, returning the Church of England to roughly its Edwardian state

1560 John a Lasco dies in Pińczów, Poland

1562 Peter Martyr Vermigli dies in Zurich, Germany

1564 Calvin dies in Geneva, Switzerland

1572 John Knox dies in Edinburgh, Scotland

1575 Heinrich Bullinger dies in Zurich, Switzerland

1611 King James Version (or Authorized Version) of the Bible completed

Confessional Statements Following the Start of the Reformation

1523	Sixty-Seven Articles of Ulrich Zwingli
1527	Schleitheim Confession
1530	Augsburg Confession
1536	Genevan Confession
1561	Belgic Confession
1563	Heidelberg Catechism
1571	Thirty-Nine Articles of the Church of England
1619	Canons of Dort
1647	Westminster Confession
1689	Second London Baptist Confession

A Pre-Reformation Hymn

Come down, O love divine,
seek thou this soul of mine,
and visit it with thine own ardour glowing;
O Comforter, draw near,
within my heart appear,
and kindle it, thy holy flame bestowing.

O let it freely burn,
till earthly passions turn
to dust and ashes in its heat consuming;
and let thy glorious light
shine ever on my sight,
and clothe me round, the while my path illuming.

Let holy charity
mine outward vesture be,
and lowliness become mine inner clothing;
true lowliness of heart,
which takes the humbler part,
and o'er its own shortcomings weeps with loathing.

And so the yearning strong,
with which the soul will long,
shall far outpass the power of human telling;
for none can guess its grace,
till he become the place
wherein the Holy Spirit makes his dwelling.

Bianco de Siena (c1350–1399)
Translated by Richard Frederick Littledale

Foreword

Lindsay Brown

I warmly welcome this short book. We have much to learn from church history, and here we see how the events of six centuries ago set the stage for the ministry of the great eighteenth- and nineteenth-century preachers like the Wesleys, George Whitefield, Jonathan Edwards, Charles Simeon, C H Spurgeon—and how they gave us the gospel now. This is not to suggest that God had left himself without a witness until the Reformation. Before the 16th century we have not only the work of Wycliffe and his followers, early martyrs, and the leadership of Jan Hus, but other glimmers of light across Europe. For example the Italian mystic poet and Jesuat, Bianco de Siena, who passed down to us the beautiful hymn 'Come down, O love divine'.

As we read Part I, looking back to the events of the Reformation, let us not miss four things.

Lindsay Brown served as IFES General Secretary from 1991 to 2007, and as International Director of the Lausanne Movement from 2008 to 2016. He is IFES Evangelist-at-Large.

First, in Luther, God used a very ordinary monk, who never lost his rough-hewn personality. His manner, and indeed his humour, could be coarse. If a church or seminary today advertised a vacancy, Luther might not make the shortlist. God is God, and he chooses servants as he will for special times.

Second, God used a movement with many strands, which stretched out over more than two hundred years, as we see in the Timeline. So while the evening of 31 October 1517 in Wittenberg is popularly regarded as 'the start of the Reformation,' it was more accurately the momentous start of its final long dénouement.

Third, it was necessary to stand against the doctrine and the authority of the church. This demanded immense courage, but the dust and grime which had accumulated over centuries in the medieval church had changed and obfuscated the message of the New Testament writers. It by now served only to obscure the truth that is in Christ Jesus; for Scripture alone is our final authority.

Fourth, the Reformation mounts a defence of the importance of doctrine. Clear understanding of biblical doctrine produces stable foundations, and gives a basis for confident belief in the redeeming work of Jesus Christ. It refreshes us spiritually like 'dew in the morning' (Deuteronomy 32:1–2) by deepening our understanding of God.

As John Stott reminds us in Part II, the Reformers were simply reaffirming what the early church

leaders, the apostles, had taught. For the evangelical
faith (far from being a deviation) is simply a *reaffir-
mation* of apostolic truth, no more and no less. The
Reformers were opening up the Scriptures to incred-
ulous eyes and showing guilt-ridden and needy people how Scripture offered them the gift of salvation
by God's grace alone through faith alone.

It has become fashionable to debunk the word
'evangelical.' True, it has been appropriated—and
abased—by some political parties. In addition, in
certain countries it is synonymous with the word
'Protestant.' But rather than rejecting it because of
this, perhaps it is time to reaffirm its meaning and
value. I recall a conversation with John Stott, who
was saddened by the misuse of the word. He told me
he was not enthusiastic about terms such as 'liberal
evangelicals,' 'conservative evangelicals,' 'generous
evangelicals,' 'open evangelical,' or 'essentially evangelical.' For he believed that the word 'evangelical'
was sufficient in itself. It is, as he explains 'a noble
word with a long and honourable history,' stretching
back as far as the second century.[4]

John Stott gives us a fine exposition of the Reformers' legacy, and of what it means for us now to
stand in that same apostolic tradition. It is in *this*
sense that the Lausanne Movement is an unashamedly evangelical movement. The term requires no

---

4. We know of its use to refer to people of 'the gospel' and
'the book' at least as far back as 180 AD, in debates between
the heretic Marcion and early Christian leaders.

particular political affiliation, nor indeed church tradition. Its root *euangelion*, the gospel, is used in the New Testament only in relation to the saving work of Christ.

The essence, then, of the gospel, is the apostolic doctrine of justification by grace alone through faith alone. This, as we see, was to be central to the Reformation. In fact, Luther is said to have summed it up as 'the article of a standing or falling church . . . it preserves and directs every doctrine of the church.'[5]

That is why Alan Purser calls us to look again at Jesus' prayer for the church. On the night Christ was betrayed, he prayed that believers would remain embedded in apostolic truth. This is what will keep us effective in mission.

It is the same power of God's grace alone, calling people to faith, that we see time and again as we survey the centuries and look around the world. I trace it clearly through the records, here in my own country, of the Welsh revivals. It is by God's grace alone that the Holy Spirit has moved in revivals in East and West Africa, and in the building of Christ's church in China, and in the many conversions we hear of in the Islamic world.

The centrality of grace was important not only to the Reformers, but we see it in the writings of Augustine, Wesley, C S Lewis. A firm grasp of grace is the foundation of deep assurance. More than that, it is the

---

5. Balthasar Meisner described this expression as 'a proverb of Luther' (*Anthropólogia sacra* disputation 24, [Wittenberg: Johannes Gormannus, 1615].

source of that much sought-after but rarely attained experience of joy. Of this truth, Luther wrote 'If you knew what you were saved from, you would die of fear, but if you knew what you are saved for, you would die of joy.'

That is why the Reformation is still not over. In our 'post-truth' generation, the message of Scripture's authority needs to be proclaimed as clearly as ever; for Scripture is true, and must be believed, obeyed, and defended, and if necessary we must be prepared to die for it.

I finish with a personal story. Some years ago, I was speaking on the doctrine of justification by grace through faith at a student conference in Argentina. It was a starry night and after speaking I went out to appreciate the stars in the Southern Hemisphere. An older man followed me. He was an elderly Dutch missionary.

'Thank you,' he said, 'for speaking about this great truth tonight. I myself have spoken on the same theme many times, and I am always deeply moved when reminded of it by others.'

'Why is that?' I inquired.

'Well,' he said, 'During the Second World War, I was a member of the Hitler Youth; I did and saw terrible things. Soon after the war, I tasted God's saving grace and I became a Christian and followed Jesus Christ. Then God called me into Christian ministry and I was sent as a pioneer missionary to Irian Jaya. There God used me in revival. On one Sunday, I baptised two thousand new believers. So, do you see why this great truth is so important to me? Because it reminds me that no trough is so deep that God cannot raise us out of it by his grace and set our feet on dry land. I deserved to be judged and cast away, but because of God's justifying grace, not only did he save me, and not only did he use me in ministry, but he saw fit to use me in revival.'

Such is the wonder of God's justifying act through the work of Christ.

May this book be used in some small way to stir the hearts of many in our generation to proclaim this message as vigorously as did the sixteenth-century Reformers.

PART I

The Story and Significance of the Reformation

Michael Reeves

A Desperate Search for Peace

The twenty-one year old was walking to his university in Erfurt, Germany, when he was caught in a sudden and violent storm. A lightning bolt hit so close it knocked him to the ground. In panic he cried out 'Saint Anne, help me! I shall become a monk!' And so the young Martin Luther began the life of a monk.

It was a life he embraced with intense seriousness. For, terrified of death and the prospect of standing before his Judge, Luther was determined to climb

Michael Reeves, President and Professor of Theology at Union School of Theology in the UK (www.ust.ac.uk), was previously Head of Theology for UCCF and an associate minister at All Souls Church, Langham Place, London. His books include *Why the Reformation Still Matters* and *The Unquenchable Flame*.

the ladder to heaven, however steep it proved. Every few hours he would leave his tiny cell and make his way to a service in the chapel, starting with matins in the middle of the night, then another at six in the morning, another at nine, another at twelve, and so on. He often took no bread or water for three days at a time, and would quite deliberately freeze himself in the winter cold in the hope that that might please God. Driven to confession, he would exhaust his confessors, taking up to six hours at a time to catalogue his most recent sins.

Yet the more he did, the more troubled he became. Was it enough? Were his motives right? Along with all his exhausting external works, he found himself sinking into an ever-deeper introspection. Then, in 1510, he was given the opportunity to visit Rome on monastery business. For him, it was a dream come true: there in Rome he could be closer to the apostles and saints than anywhere else. The place was crammed with their relics, and each one, he had been taught, conferred various spiritual benefits. On arrival, he dashed manically from holy site to holy site, hoping to clock up merit at each. He actually wished his parents were dead so that he could have freed them from purgatory by virtue of all the merit he was amassing.

Then he decided to climb the Scala Sancta. This was the staircase which, supposedly, Jesus had climbed to appear before Pilate, and which had subsequently been brought to Rome. Kissing each step as he climbed, and repeating the Lord's Prayer for each one, he was assured he could free the soul of his choice from purgatory. Of course, he ran at the chance. Yet on reaching the top he was forced to ask 'Who knows whether it is true?'

On his return, Luther was transferred to the Augustinian monastery in the tiny town of Wittenberg. The place may have been small, but it was the capital of Electoral Saxony, and the regional ruler, Frederick 'the Wise', had made it the home of his stunning collection of relics. There in the Castle Church, the pilgrim could enjoy nine aisles crammed with more than nineteen thousand relics. Highlights included a wisp of straw from Christ's crib, a strand of his beard, a nail from the cross, a piece of bread from the Last Supper, a twig from Moses' burning bush, a few of Mary's hairs and some bits of her clothing, as well as innumerable teeth and bones from celebrated saints. More to the point, veneration of each piece was worth an indulgence of one hundred days (with a bonus one for each aisle), meaning the pious visitor could tot up more than 1,900,000 days off purgatory.

The Purgatory Industry

Purgatory and indulgences are not familiar concepts to everyone today, but they sprang from the teaching that few would die righteous enough to merit salvation fully. So unless Christians died unrepentant of a 'mortal' sin such as murder (in which case they would go to hell), they had the chance *after* death to have all their sins slowly *purged* from them in *purg*atory. Then they could enter heaven, fully cleansed. Few relished the prospect of thousands, or even millions, of years of chastisement after death, and sought to fast-track the route through purgatory, both for themselves and for those they loved. As well as prayers said for the dead, whole services of mass could be said for souls in purgatory. The grace of that mass could then be applied directly to the departed and tormented soul.

An entire industry evolved around purgatory for exactly this reason. The wealthy founded chantries, which were special chapels with priests dedicated to saying prayers and masses for the soul of their sponsor or his fortunate beneficiaries; the less wealthy clubbed together in fraternities to pay for the same.

Most people, then, could expect a stint in purgatory after death. But Luther had been taught that there were saints who had been so good that, not only had they enough merit to enter heaven direct, bypassing purgatory altogether, they actually had *more* merit than they needed. This 'spare merit' of theirs was kept, as it were, in the church's treasury, to which only the pope had the keys. The pope could therefore give a gift of merit (an indulgence) to any soul he deemed worthy, fast-tracking that soul's path through purgatory, or even leap-frogging purgatory altogether (with a 'full,' or 'plenary' indulgence). By Luther's day, a donation of money to the church was often deemed penitential enough to merit such an indulgence. Thus it became increasingly clear in people's minds: a bit of cash could secure spiritual bliss. To a monk like Brother Martin, such easy religious trading made a mockery of true repentance. It was a scandal waiting to happen.

Then Luther heard about Johann Tetzel. Tetzel was an indulgence-monger with a lurid style and a travelling quartet. He advertised the indulgences with such jingles as 'When the coin in the coffer rings, the soul from purgatory springs,' and asked his audiences 'Don't you hear the voices of your wailing dead parents and others, who say, "Have mercy on me, because we are in severe punishment and pain. From this you could redeem us with a small alms."?' He did not even ask people to confess their sins. Just the money would do.

On All Saints' Day (1 November), 1517, the merits of the saints were due to be offered in Wittenberg, and Luther saw it as a chance to debate the issue. So, on 31 October (All Saints' Eve) he nailed to the door of the Castle Church a list of ninety-five theses for debate over the matter of indulgences. Everyone would have to see it the next day. In it he asked questions such as why the pope does not release all souls from purgatory out of love, instead of charging for it. But most significantly, he addressed the practice of procuring indulgences, for they effectively replaced the need for true repentance of the heart with a mere external transaction. Supporting this argument, he soon found that the proof text from the Latin Vulgate which was used to validate the sacrament of penance was a mistranslation of the original Greek. In the Vulgate, Matthew 4:17 read *penitentiam agite* ('do penance'), whereas the Greek meant 'change your mind,' something internal and not merely external.

Luther could never have predicted the consequences of his action, for, unintentionally, he had started a chain reaction that would turn Europe upside down. The first reaction came, unsurprisingly, from Johann Tetzel. He immediately issued thunderous demands for Luther to be burned as a heretic, and the clamour against Luther only grew. Soon Luther was having to debate far more skilled theologians, and it became increasingly clear that the real issue was one of authority. Which had the final say: the church, or the Bible?

Entering Paradise Itself

During all this time of tumult, Luther's own understanding of Christianity was shifting. He had posted his ninety-five theses because he believed that indulgences cheapened repentance. But the more he thought about it, the more he saw how superficially he himself had been treating sin. In his schooling he had heard the theologians say that 'God will not deny grace to those who do their best.' As a result, he had seen his sin as an outward, behavioural problem—a problem that could be corrected with better conduct. Now, however, he was increasingly aware that the real problem is far deeper: sin is in our hearts, shaping the very grain of our desires. Those who 'do their best' are therefore still only acting out the sin that is in their hearts by depending on themselves in their sinful self-love. And that being the case, improved behaviour and religious action will not help. We do not need improved performance, but new hearts.

Yet while his sense of sin deepened, for a long time his understanding of the grace of God did not. For years Luther could only see that God was all Judge and no love, his righteousness being all about punishing sinners, his 'gospel' just the promise of judgment. Here was a God he could only ever cower before. 'Though I lived as a monk without reproach,' he wrote,

> I felt that I was a sinner before God with an extremely disturbed conscience. I could not believe that he was placated by my satisfaction. I did not love, yes, I hated the righteous God who punishes sinners, and secretly, if not blasphemously, certainly murmuring greatly, I was angry with God, and said, "As if, indeed, it is not enough, that miserable sinners, eternally lost through original sin, are crushed by every kind of calamity by the law of the decalogue, without having God add pain to pain by the gospel and also by the gospel threatening us with his righ-

teousness and wrath!" Thus I raged with a fierce
and troubled conscience.'[6]

All that anguish only pushed him, in his cell in the
monastery tower, to study the Scriptures harder. Particularly, he wanted to know what Paul could possi-
bly mean by the phrase 'the righteousness of God' in
Romans 1:17.

> At last, by the mercy of God, meditating day and
> night, I gave heed to the context of the words,
> namely, "In it the righteousness of God is re-
> vealed, as it is written, 'He who through faith is
> righteous shall live.'" There I began to understand
> that the righteousness of God is that by which the
> righteous lives by a gift of God, namely by faith.
> And this is the meaning: the righteousness of God
> is revealed by the gospel, namely, the passive righ-
> teousness with which merciful God justifies us
> by faith, as it is written, "He who through faith
> is righteous shall live." Here I felt that I was alto-
> gether born again and had entered paradise itself
> through open gates.[7]

---

6. Martin Luther, *Luther's Works, Vol. 34: Career of the
Reformer IV*, ed. Jaroslav Jan Pelikan, Hilton C Oswald, and
Helmut T Lehmann (Philadelphia: Fortress Press, 1999),
336–37.

7. Martin Luther, *Luther's Works, Vol. 34: Career of the
Reformer IV*, ed. Jaroslav Jan Pelikan, Hilton C Oswald, and
Helmut T Lehmann (Philadelphia: Fortress Press, 1999), 337.

With this, Luther had discovered an entirely different God and the entirely different way he relates to
us. The righteousness of God, the glory of God, the
wisdom of God: these are not ways in which God is
against us. These are things God has that he shares
with us. Here Luther saw for the first time truly good
news of a kind and generous God who gives sinners
the gift of his own righteousness. The Christian
life, then, could not be about the sinner's struggle
to achieve his own, paltry, human righteousness; it
was about accepting God's own, perfect, divine righteousness. Here now was a God who does not want
our goodness but our trust. Forgiveness did not de-
pend on how certain the sinner is that he has been
truly contrite; forgiveness comes simply by receiving
the promise of God. Thus the sinner's hope is found,
not in himself, but outside himself, in God's word of
promise. All the struggles and all the anxiety could
be replaced with massive confidence and simple faith.

When (in 1520) Luther came to explain his dis-
covery to the world in a little tract called *The Freedom
of a Christian*, he used a beautiful and revealing illus-
tration. The gospel, he explained, is like the story of
a king (representing Jesus) who married a prostitute
(representing a sinner). No works of hers could ever
win her the right to be his bride. However, when the
king made his marriage vow, the prostitute became, by
status, a queen. It is not that she made her behaviour
queenly and thus made herself the queen. Indeed, she
did not know how to behave as befits royalty. But he
changed her *status* when he took her to be his. Thus

she found herself to be still her poor old self at heart, and at the same time a queen by status.

Just so, the sinner, on accepting Christ's promise in the gospel, is simultaneously (i) a sinner at heart and (ii) righteous by status. The Christian is at the same time righteous and a sinner (*simul justus et peccator*), and will always remain so (*semper justus et peccator*). For by God's grace Christians have a righteousness credited to them that is not their own: the righteousness of Christ. As Luther put it, we have a righteousness that is both alien (external, and not our own) and passive (unearned). What has happened is the 'joyful exchange' in which all that the believer has (her sin) she gives to Christ, and all that he has (his righteousness, blessedness, life, and glory) he gives to her.

> Her sins cannot now destroy her, since they are laid upon Christ and swallowed up by him. And she has that righteousness in Christ, her husband, of which she may boast as of her own and which she can confidently display alongside her sins in the face of death and hell and say, "If I have sinned, yet my Christ, in whom I believe, has not sinned, and all his is mine and all mine is his," as the bride in the Song of Solomon [2:16] says, "My beloved is mine and I am his."[8]

---

8. Martin Luther, *Luther's Works, Vol. 31: Career of the Reformer I*, ed. Jaroslav Jan Pelikan, Hilton C Oswald, and Helmut T Lehmann (Philadelphia: Fortress Press, 1999), 352.

Here I Stand

Luther was soon summoned to a session (or 'diet') of the imperial court in Worms, where most assumed he would soon be burned for heresy. When he arrived he was initially so intimidated by the questioning in the presence of all the rulers and nobility that he could hardly speak. The papal nuncio took Luther to be too stupid to have written all that he had, and wanted to know who really was behind the Reformation tracts. After an order to recant, came Luther's final answer:

> I am bound by the Scriptures I have quoted and my conscience is captive to the Word of God. I cannot and I will not retract anything, since it is neither safe nor right to go against conscience. I cannot do otherwise, here I stand, may God help me, Amen.[9]

It did not take long for the emperor to declare Luther to be 'an obstinate schismatic and manifest heretic' who should be harboured by none and read by none, on pain of the direst punishment. Luther, however, was not waiting around in Worms to be condemned. He had already boarded a wagon for Wittenberg.

Then he simply disappeared. What was clear was that he had been abducted from the wagon by armed

---

9. Martin Luther, *Luther's Works, Vol. 32: Career of the Reformer II*, ed. Jaroslav Jan Pelikan, Hilton C Oswald, and Helmut T Lehmann (Philadelphia: Fortress Press, 1999), 112–13.

horsemen; what was not clear was what then happened to him. Most assumed he had been seized for a quiet and summary execution. In fact the kidnappers were in the employ of Frederick the Wise, who had devised the plan to keep Luther in safe custody without incurring the dangers of being seen to harbour an outlaw. Under cover of night, Luther had been secretly escorted to the Wartburg Castle, Frederick's stronghold in Electoral Saxony.

The castle was Luther's covert home for the next ten months. He let his hair and beard grow, and introduced himself to people as 'Sir George.' Most remarkably, though, there in hiding, and in less than eleven weeks, he managed to translate the Greek New Testament into German. Amazingly, in that short period Luther managed to produce a masterpiece of a translation. The language was so punchy, so colourful, so of-the-street, that it transformed the very way people spoke German. Luther was becoming the father of the modern German language. More importantly, with its publication in September 1522, Luther realised his dream that the people 'might seize and taste the clear, pure Word of God itself and hold to it.'

It was not a happy time there, however. Cooped up in hiding, Luther suffered from a plague of doubts. Yet it is revealing how he battled them. Often he would write out a relevant Bible verse on his wall, on a piece of furniture, or, indeed, anything to hand. The point was that he knew that within himself there was only sin and doubt. All his hope lay outside himself, in God's word. There his security before God was unaffected by how he felt or how he did. And so, when facing doubt, he would not look within himself for any comfort; instead, he would hold before his eyes this unchanging, external word.

For the next quarter of a century, until his death in 1546, Luther lived in Wittenberg promoting the reformation of the church in sermons, catechisms, books, hymns, and conversations. Perhaps best-known among his hymns was that battle hymn of the Reformation, 'A Mighty Fortress is our God,' the words of which made his ideas familiar to millions:

> The Prince of Darkness grim,
> we tremble not for him;
> His rage we can endure,
> for lo, his doom is sure,
> One little word shall fell him.

To the very end of his life Luther had a red-blooded and brawny personality. Some loved it, others wished he could be at least a little less rude and raw. Certainly he was no stained-glass ideal. Perhaps, though, such a blunt man was just what was needed for the seemingly impossible task of challenging all Christendom and turning it around. He was shock therapy for the world. And, somehow, his personality seemed fit for the gospel he uncovered: he inspired no moral self-improvement in would-be disciples; instead, his evident humanity testified to a sinner's absolute need for God's grace.

Three Critical Players: Erasmus, Wycliffe, and Tyndale

Essential to Luther's story was the work of the great humanist scholar, Erasmus. In 1516, Erasmus had published a critical new Greek edition of the New Testament. Before that, most people had known only the official Latin Vulgate translation that the church used. Erasmus opened up direct study of the original Greek text—and men like Luther found a message in it that had never been clear in the Latin.

But it wasn't just Luther. In Britain also, scholars were soon being transformed by what they read in the Greek. A century and a half earlier, an Oxford scholar named John Wycliffe had organized a translation of the Latin Vulgate Bible into English, and his followers were still eagerly reading their Bibles and preaching. But what those who could read found in Erasmus' edition was something else. And even those who couldn't read it were soon coming across copies of Luther's books, which had started pouring into the country. In Cambridge, one group of dons was known to gather at the White Horse Inn, where all the Luther-talk made it look so like Wittenberg that it was soon nicknamed 'Little Germany.'

One such scholar was the brilliant young linguist, William Tyndale. Inspired by his study of the New Testament, he concluded 'It was impossible to establish the lay people in any truth, except the Scripture were laid before their eyes in their mother tongue.'[10] He therefore set about his life's work of translating the Bible from its original Greek and Hebrew into English. He sailed for Germany, making his way to Worms; and there, where just five years earlier Luther had made his 'Here I stand' speech in front of the emperor, Tyndale published his complete New Testament in English.

For over a hundred years, the followers of John Wycliffe had produced and read translations of the New Testament in English, but they were only handwritten, rather wooden renditions of the Latin Vulgate. They were impossible to mass-produce, and still contained all the theological problems of the Latin ('do penance' instead of 'repent,' for example). Tyndale's New Testament, however, could and would be printed off by the thousands, then smuggled into England in bales of cloth, and soon accompanied by his *Parable of the Wicked Mammon*, an argument for justification through faith alone. Even more importantly, Tyndale's New Testament was a gem of a translation. Accurate and beautifully written, it was a page-turner.

Eventually the wrath of the church caught up with Tyndale, but not before he had managed to translate a good portion of the Old Testament, and some sixteen thousand copies of his Bible had been

---

10. William Tyndale, 'The Preface of Master William Tyndale, That He Made Before the Five Books of Moses, Called Genesis,' in *The Works of William Tyndale* (1848; repr., Edinburgh: Banner of Truth, 2010), 394.

smuggled into England. This was an incredible feat, given a population of at most 2.5 million, which was largely illiterate. In 1535 he was caught, and the following October he was officially strangled and burned near Brussels, his immortal last words 'Lord, open the King of England's eyes!'

That 'King of England' was Henry VIII, a ruler whose loathing of Luther had only deepened down through the years, when the Reformer opposed the annulment of his marriage. Indeed, for opposing Luther the pope had awarded the king the title 'Defender of the Faith.' He hardly seemed a bright hope for the Reformation. And yet, just two years after Tyndale had died uttering that prayer, it was decreed that an English Bible be placed in every church in the land. In 1538, the king ordered that 'ye shall discourage no man from the reading or hearing of the Bible, but shall expressly provoke, stir and exhort every person to read the same as that which is the very lively word of God.'[11]

Six English Bibles were placed in St Paul's Cathedral, crowds immediately thronging round those who could read loud enough to make themselves heard. So great was the excitement that priests complained of how, even during the sermon, laypeople were reading the Bible aloud to each other. Private Bible-reading became a much more widespread feature of ordinary life, as even the illiterate learnt to

---

11. The Second Royal injunctions of Henry VIII, item 3.

read, so as to gain immediate access to 'the very lively word of God.'

The Fiery Trial of the Martyrs

The reformation of the church by the word of God never was—and never could be—a smooth road. When King Henry VIII of England died in 1547, just under a year after Luther, Reformers were filled with hope because of his evangelical son and heir, the new King Edward VI. They were not disappointed: Edward presided over a comprehensive period of reformation in England. Church services were made evangelical in content, preaching was commanded in English, and many notable reformed preachers started to become household names. But within six years it was all over: Edward VI died and was succeeded by his arch-Catholic half-sister, Mary, who would undo all he had achieved. (He had expressed a wish that he be succeeded by his Protestant first cousin, Lady Jane Gray, but she was to be deposed by Mary after a mere nine days.)

As quickly as she could, Mary returned England to Roman Catholicism. Evangelical bishops were removed from office, Bibles were removed from churches, and Roman Catholic worship was restored. Many evangelicals sought refuge abroad; others decided to stay and operate quietly, secretly distributing their 'naughty books' and meeting in (often quite large) underground congregations. Those who stayed and did not lie low were imprisoned and burned. In all, and in stark contrast to the tolerance of Edward's reign, Mary's reign saw some three hundred evangelicals burned for their faith, not counting the many others who died in the horrendous conditions of sixteenth-century prisons.

Among Mary's most famous victims were the old Archbishop of Canterbury, Thomas Cranmer; the famous preacher and Bishop of Worcester, Hugh Latimer; and the Bishop of London, Nicholas Ridley. In October 1555, Ridley and Latimer were burned together, back to back, at the end of Broad Street in Oxford.[12] Latimer, aged about eighty, was the first to die, shouting through the flames 'Be of good comfort, Master Ridley, and play the man; we shall this day light such a candle, by God's grace, in England, as I trust shall never be put out.' Unfortunately for Ridley the wood had been badly laid around him so that he suffered terribly, his legs burning off before the rest of him was touched. The horrible sight apparently moved hundreds to tears.

Five months later in March 1556 Thomas Cranmer was burned on the same spot. The old Archbishop and architect of so much of the English Reformation, now nearly seventy, had, under extreme duress, renounced his Protestantism. It was a triumph for Mary's reign. Despite his recantation, however, he was such an embodiment of the Reformation that it was decided he should be burned in any case. It was

---

12. A cross, in cobbles, still marks the place.

a decision that would more than undo Mary's victory, for when the day came, Cranmer refused to read out his recantation. Instead he stated boldly that he was indeed a Protestant, though a cowardly one for forsaking his principles. In consequence, he announced, 'for as much as my hand offended, writing contrary to my heart, my hand shall first be punished there-for.' He was true to his word: as the fires were lit, he held out the hand that had signed his recantation so that it might burn first. Having briefly denied his Protestantism, Cranmer thus burned with movingly defiant bravery; and so died the first Protestant Archbishop of Canterbury.

John Calvin: Reforming the World

In 1509, a few short years before Luther made his stand, John Calvin, the Reformation's second-most-significant leader, was born in northern France. As a young student, Calvin soon found himself mixing with a group of scholars who were often sympathetic to some idea of church reformation. He even began learning Greek, which by the 1520s had an edgy reputation as the language of the Reformation. Perhaps he read some of Luther's writings. At any rate, he wrote that around this time 'God by a sudden conversion subdued and brought my mind to a teachable frame.'

Meanwhile, France was becoming an ever more dangerous place for reformers. Calvin's name was blacklisted and soon he was on the run. He decided to make his way to Strasbourg via Geneva, a city that had recently allied itself to the Reformation. Calvin had no intention of staying in Geneva, but he was waylaid by the fiery Guillaume Farel, instigator of the Reformation there. Farel then asked God to curse Calvin if he did not stay and assist him in the urgent work of reformation there. Terrified, the young scholar agreed to remain.

It was a momentous meeting, for Calvin would dedicate the rest of his life (bar a short exile) to Geneva, turning it into a world centre of evangelicalism. One important early step was the submission to the city council of a list of proposals for the comprehensive reformation of the church in Geneva. Most were accepted. He proposed, among other things, that every household should receive a pastoral visit every year, and that everyone should learn the new catechism that explained the evangelical faith. The proposals are revealing, for they make it clear that Reformation was not about simply breaking from Rome; it meant dedication to ongoing reform by the word. The reformed church must be always reforming.

Evangelicals from across Europe—and especially from persecuted regions—began flocking to Geneva. Yet while they were warmly welcomed, Calvin did not want Geneva to be so much a refuge as a seedbed for the spread of the gospel. Thus in 1555 he established a top-secret programme for the evangelization of his native France. He was already well-established as the leader-in-exile of French Protestantism, in regular contact with many of the underground churches there. But now a secret network was set up, with safe houses and hiding places, so agents of the gospel could be slipped across the border into France to plant new churches (sometimes literally underground). With secret printing presses installed in Paris and Lyons to resource them, it was a stunning success. Demand for the literature soon far outstripped what the presses could supply, and printing became the dominant industry in Geneva in an attempt to cope with the need.

More than ten percent of the entire population of France became reformed, with some two million or more gathering in the hundreds of newly planted churches. Calvinism, as it became known, fared especially well among the nobility, roughly a third of whom appear to have converted, giving the reformed faith a political clout disproportionate to its actual size. Calvin wrote a confession of faith for the church there in 1559, and supported them in whatever way he could. Despite the growth of evangelicalism in France, encouragement was desperately needed: for example, when one church was raided in Paris, more than a hundred believers were arrested and seven burned. And, while he wrote from a position of freedom to fortify them, he never spoke as though from an ivory tower. His letters are splattered everywhere with mentions of the blood he was sure he would soon have to shed as, in Geneva, he felt the imminent threat of martyrdom.

Calvin was, quite deliberately, doing all he could to turn Geneva into an international centre for the propagation of the gospel. He advised Protestant rulers from Scotland to Italy; he trained refugees who came to Geneva and then returned to their native countries; and he dispatched missionaries to Poland, Hungary, the Netherlands, Italy, even South America. The real engine room for all this was the college and academy Calvin opened in the city in 1559. Starting with a general education and moving on to a detailed study of theology and books of the Bible, it equipped the pastors, who could then be dispatched, fully armed and trained.

Teaching and preaching was for Calvin the heart of the Reformation, as it was for Luther. Calvin devoted most of his time to this, lecturing three times a week, preaching twice each Sunday and, on alternate weeks, every weekday as well. Publishing became a priority, and through amalgamating his lectures, he managed to produce commentaries on nearly every book of the Bible, so as to help preachers elsewhere. These were a very different sort of commentary from what Europe had known before: their aim was 'an easy brevity that does not involve obscurity.' As a result of his 'sudden conversion,' Calvin had become convinced that God brings life and new life into being only through his word. Proclaiming this became the essence of his life's work.

What Was at the Heart
of the Reformation?

From the moment Luther understood from Romans 1 that God's righteousness is an entirely unmerited gift, he saw this as the most important truth in the world. Justification was at the heart of the Reformation; its essential matter.

By 'justification' Reformers like Luther and Calvin meant a divine declaration that the righteousness of Christ is imputed to the believer because of God's grace alone (*sola gratia*). This justification is therefore through faith alone (*sola fide*) in Christ alone, meaning that all the glory of salvation goes to God alone and not us. 'Nothing in this article [of faith] can be given up or compromised,' wrote Luther, 'even if heaven and earth and things temporal should be destroyed.' It is the belief, he said, 'on which the church stands or falls.'

Not everybody grasped this as Luther did, but Luther's experience with Romans 1 was to be the central thread of the Reformation: and it was through the Bible that this essential matter of justification was discovered. Justification was what made the Reformation the Reformation. And for those who accepted that God freely declares sinners to be righteous, it was a doctrine of comfort and joy. As William Tyndale put it, '*Euangelion* (that we call the gospel) is a Greek word and signifieth good, merry, glad and joyful tidings, that maketh a man's heart

glad and maketh him sing, dance, and leap for joy.'[13]
Luther too felt that by it he was 'altogether born again
and had entered paradise itself through open gates.'
And no wonder: the fact that he, a failing sinner, was
perfectly loved by God because he was clothed with
the very righteousness of Christ himself gave him a
dazzling confidence. As he counselled a friend,

> When the devil throws our sins up to us and de-
> clares that we deserve death and hell, we ought
> to speak thus: 'I admit that I deserve death and
> hell. What of it? Does this mean that I shall be
> sentenced to eternal damnation? By no means.
> For I know One who suffered and made satisfac-
> tion in my behalf. His name is Jesus Christ, the
> Son of God. Where he is, there I shall be also.'[14]

It is hardly as though the significance of this
message has diminished down through the years.
Today we are bombarded with the message that we
will be more loved when we make ourselves more
attractive. It may not be God-related, and yet still it is
a religion of works, and one that is deeply embedded.
For that, the Reformation has the most sparkling
good news. As Luther put it: 'sinners are attractive

---

13. 'A Pathway into Holy Scripture,' in *The Works of William Tyndale* (Edinburgh & Carlisle, PA: Banner of Truth,
2010), 1:8.

14. To Jerome Weller, July 1530, in *Luther: Letters of Spiritual Counsel*, Library of Christian Classics, T G Tappert, ed.
(Vancouver: Regent College, 2003), p. 86–87.

because they are loved; they are not loved because they are attractive.'[15]

If justification by faith alone was the essential *matter* of the Reformation, the supreme authority of the Bible was its *medium*. To achieve substantial reformation, it took Luther's attitude that Scripture is the only sure foundation for belief (*sola Scriptura*). The Bible had to be acknowledged as the supreme authority, and allowed to contradict and overrule all other claims, or else it would itself be overruled. In other words, a simple reverence for the Bible and acknowledgement that it has some authority would never have been enough to bring about the Reformation. *Sola Scriptura* was the indispensable key for profound and healthy change.

Is the Reformation Still Significant?

If the Reformation were merely a negative reaction to a purely historical problem, then it would not be significant for evangelicals today. But the closer one looks, the clearer it becomes: the Reformation was not, principally, a negative movement, about moving away from Rome; it was a positive movement, about moving towards the gospel. And

---

15. Martin Luther, *Luther's Works, Vol. 31: Career of the Reformer I*, ed. Jaroslav Jan Pelikan, Hilton C Oswald, and Helmut T Lehmann (Philadelphia: Fortress Press, 1999), 57.

to move towards the gospel meant unearthing original, scriptural, apostolic Christianity by then buried under centuries of human tradition. That is what preserves the validity of the Reformation for today. For the church must always be reforming and constantly moving ever closer to the gospel. This is encapsulated in two words we often hear: '*semper reformanda.*' But their context is important, for the full Latin phrase is: *Ecclesia reformata et semper reformanda secundum verbum Dei* ('The church reformed and always reforming *according to the Word of God.*'). The Reformation cannot be over. It must be an evangelical banner, borne with both humility and resolution.

For evangelicals, this is our story. It is a story of brave and eloquent witnesses to the truth of God's grace found in his word. And as much as it is our story, it must also be our standard. May God grant us the brave faithfulness of the Reformers to work together in evangelical unity for the ongoing reformation and growth of his church!

PART II

Keep the Faith and Pass It On

What Is the Evangelical Faith and Why Does It Matter?

John Stott

I. What Is the Evangelical Faith?

First, what is the evangelical faith? At the risk of oversimplification I want to argue that the evangelical faith is nothing other than the historic Christian faith: original, biblical, apostolic Christianity. The evangelical Christian seeks by the grace of God to be faithful to the revelation which God has given of himself in Christ and in Scripture. 'Evangelical' is a noble word, with a long and honorable history. We bear it with humility and with thankfulness.

John Stott, Chief Architect of the Lausanne Covenant, was Honorary Vice President of the Lausanne Movement. He wrote over fifty books, and was founder of what is now Langham Partnership International, which works to strengthen the Church in the Majority World.

Of course we recognise that we are not the only Christians in the world. There are large numbers of other people who profess to follow Jesus Christ, who call themselves 'Catholic' or 'Orthodox' or 'liberal Protestant.' Insofar as they profess Jesus Christ as God, Lord, and Saviour, we certainly do not deny them the Christian name. To be sure we don't agree with everything they believe. At some points we find ourselves in sharp disagreement with them. We also remember that not all those who claim to belong to Christ in fact do so, because nominal Christianity is a tragic phenomenon in every church.

At the same time we must learn to distinguish between principles on the one hand and personalities on the other. We can reject a person's doctrine without rejecting the person, and we must learn to make that distinction. We need to respect people we disagree with, to meet them, love them, talk to them, and listen to them, because we don't claim to be omniscient or infallible. We can cooperate with them in works of Christian compassion and social justice. It is when we are invited to evangelize with them that we find ourselves in a painful dilemma, for common witness necessitates common faith, and an agreement over the content of the *evangel*.

What we evangelicals want to be is plain, Bible Christians. This is why our claiming that the evangelical faith is the historic Christian faith is not the arrogant claim it may sound, although it has sometimes been put forward in an arrogant way. If it can be shown that we have misunderstood or distorted the biblical message whether by addition or by subtraction, whether by manipulation or by deviation, then we must be ready and eager immediately to change. Our aim, in humility, is to be loyal to the biblical revelation.

'Renovators, Not Innovators'

The sixteenth-century reformers who gave currency to the term 'evangelical' and to whom we look back with enormous gratitude and admiration, were quite clear that the evangelical faith is the Christian faith in its original and authentic form. The leaders of the Roman Catholic church at that time accused them of inventing and introducing a new faith. On the contrary, they replied, we are recovering the old faith.

Luther wrote: 'We teach no new thing, but we repeat and establish old things which the apostles and all godly teachers have taught before us.'[16] Hugh Latimer declared: 'You say it is a new learning; now I tell you it is the old learning.'[17] And John Jewel, Bishop of Salisbury from 1560, in his great and fa-

---

16. Commentary on the Apostle Paul's Epistle to the Galatians (Chapter 1:4a).

17. He continued strikingly: 'Ye say it is old heresy, new scoured. Nay, I tell you it is old truth, long rusted with your canker, and now made bright and scoured.' (In *The Politics of the Public Sphere in Early Modern England* by Peter Lake and Steven Pincus).

mous *Apology* wrote: 'It is not our doctrine that we bring you this day. We wrote it not out, we are not the inventors of it. We bring you nothing but what the old fathers of the church, what the apostles, what Christ our Saviour himself has brought before us.'[18] Then Lancelot Andrewes at the beginning of the seventeenth century coined the epigram: 'We are renovators, not innovators.'[19]

How then shall I summarise the evangelical faith? Many creeds, confessions, and catechisms have been composed through the centuries, for there is no one way to formulate the historic Christian faith. The most widely acceptable has been the Apostles' Creed. It is given in a Trinitarian structure with paragraphs concerning belief in God the Father, the Son, and the Holy Spirit. I propose to use this as an outline, because evangelical Christians are Trinitarian Christians. At the same time, I will try to fill it out, because some vital doctrines (such as the atonement and the nature of salvation) are not included in it.

---

18. *Apology of the Church of England*, 1562.
19. Scholar and Bishop of Chichester, Ely, then Winchester, who oversaw the translation of the King James Version (also known as the Authorized Version) of the Bible.

Our Trinitarian Faith

We believe in God the Father.

I will subdivide this belief into three:

1. *God the Father is the God of Creation.* Whatever means he employed in the creation (and there is room for continuing debate) we are all agreed that God created everything by his will and word. The climax of his creative purpose and process is humankind, male and female, bearing his image and sharing his dominion over the earth and its creatures. So all things owe their origin and their continuance to God. He is the Supreme Reality within and behind all that can be apprehended by our five senses. In him we live and move and have our being. We find our humanness—what it means to be an authentic and liberated human being—only in knowing him, loving him, worshipping him, and obeying him, in whose image we have been made.

2. *The God of creation is the God of the Covenant.* While all human beings fell through disobedience, and became rebels under the just judgment of God, God in his grace did not abandon them for their wilfulness. On the contrary he immediately promised to rescue, redeem, even recreate them. So the

plan of divine salvation began, culminating in our Lord and Saviour Jesus Christ. First God called Abraham and made a covenant with him, promising not only to be his God and to bless him, but through him to bless all the families of the earth.[20] God has kept his promise, first in the children of Israel, his covenant people, whose bittersweet story is told in the pages of the Old Testament. And now in us, people of his new covenant, sealed by the blood of Jesus, a covenant incorporating now not Jews only, but believers from every nation, in fulfilment of God's promise to Abraham. All who share Abraham's faith share also in Abraham's blessings.

3. *The God of creation and of the covenant is also the God of Revelation.* God reveals himself through his creation. 'The heavens declare the glory of God' and 'the whole earth is full of his glory' (Psalm 19:1; Isaiah 6:3). But to his covenant people God has given a special revelation, a revelation of his loving plan to save sinners. You cannot learn that plan of salvation by contemplating the stars. You can read the glory of God in the stars, but you cannot read the love and salvation of God through Christ in the stars. A special revelation was needed, a revelation given by mighty acts of

---

20. Genesis 12:2, 3.

salvation in redeeming Israel, but supremely in his mightiest-of-all acts, the death and resurrection of Jesus. This was a revelation given also in words—through the prophets in the Old Testament and the apostles in the New Testament who were called to record and explain what God was doing in his mighty acts. It is a revelation that is now preserved as 'the Bible.'

The immeasurable blessing of the Bible is that it makes accessible to us (every day and in every place) what God has said and done in Jesus. Without the Bible we should know practically nothing about Jesus. So we could not come to him to put our trust in him, and so we could not be saved. Thank God for the Bible! Its overriding purpose is to bring Jesus to us, and us to Jesus. It bears authoritative witness to him as the Saviour we poor sinners need, the Saviour who died for us and rose again. It unfolds the way of salvation through Christ, how we can be justified, sanctified, and glorified. It invites us to come to him, rely on him, obey him, grow up into maturity in him, work for him on earth, and wait for him from heaven. All these things are found in the Bible which witnesses to Jesus Christ.

We believe in God the Father.

We believe in God the Son.

In particular, we believe in Christ's absolute uniqueness. I subdivide it again.

1. *Christ is unique in his person.* Jesus of Nazareth is the Word made flesh, the eternal Son of God incarnate. Evangelical Christians are unashamedly committed to the historic Christian faith about the two natures of the one Person, Jesus Christ—his full deity derived in eternity from his Father, and his real humanity derived in time from his virgin mother. And we see in the gospels ample evidence for both. There has never been anybody like him, and there never will be again.

2. *He is unique in his work.* Having lived the perfect life of love and obedience, he went voluntarily and deliberately to the cross. Without any sin or sins of his own, he 'bore our sins in his own body on the tree' (1 Peter 2:24). That is, he endured in his own innocent person the consequences our sins deserved. The death he died was the just penalty for sin—not his sins, for he had none, but ours, with which he had identified himself. By becoming our substitute, taking our place and dying our death, he perfectly satisfied both the justice and the love of God. Not that he did something God the Father was unwilling to do. On

the contrary, God was in Christ doing it, in his justice demanding—and in his love providing—a perfect sacrifice for sin. Then on the third day he rose again. Or rather, he *was raised* by the Father to demonstrate publicly and powerfully the glory of his Person and the finished nature of his work; and to exalt him to that place of supreme honour at the right hand of the Father, the place of power and authority from which he is able to save today.

3. *He is unique in the salvation he offers.* Because of the unique person Jesus is and because of the unique work that he did, he is able to offer a unique salvation to all who repent and believe.

Those are the three uniquenesses of Jesus, the one and only God-man, who made the one and only perfect sacrifice for sin, who is the one and only mediator between God and us (1 Timothy 2:5). Nobody else is able to do this. As Peter put it, 'neither is there salvation in any other, for there is no other name under heaven given among men whereby we must be saved' (Acts 4:12).

We believe in God the Son, and in his three-fold uniqueness.

We believe in God the Holy Spirit.

This time I will subdivide by reference to five of the Holy Spirit's many titles in the New Testament.

1. *He is the Spirit of life.* As the Nicene Creed puts it, 'We believe in the Holy Spirit, the Lord, the Life-giver.' From our standpoint the Christian life begins when we repent and believe in Jesus. But from God's it begins when we who were dead in trespasses and sins are brought to new life by a new birth from the Spirit of life. To be born again is to be born from above, to be born of the Spirit. It is the Holy Spirit who gives us a new life, a new nature, a new outlook, new aspirations, and new ambitions. For 'if anybody is in Christ, he is a new creation, the old things have passed away, behold new things have come' (2 Corinthians 5:17). He is the Spirit of life.

2. *He is the Spirit of truth.* Dwelling now personally within us, he counters the slanders of that great liar, the devil; he assures us by his inward witness that we are God's beloved children; and he teaches us out of God's word so that we grow in our knowledge of God.

3. *He is the Spirit of holiness*—the Holy Spirit. His great desire is to transform us continuously from one degree of glory to another

into the image of Christ (2 Corinthians 3:18). The Spirit of Christ wants to form Christ in us, and to cause to ripen in our character his beautiful fruits of love, joy, peace, patience, kindness, goodness, gentleness, faithfulness, and self-control (Galatians 5:22, 23).

4. *He is the Spirit of unity.* The one Spirit creates the one body (Ephesians 4:3, 4). He binds us together in the Christian fellowship. His first fruit is love. He also equips us with evangelistic and pastoral gifts in order that the body of Christ may grow, and he empowers us to witness in the world.

5. *He is the Spirit of glory.* As Peter wrote 'The Spirit of glory rests upon you' (1 Peter 3:14). The indwelling Spirit is the first instalment of God's complete salvation, his personal pledge that the rest will follow in the end. The Holy Spirit will deliver not only our bodies but the whole universe out of its bondage to decay into the liberty of glory (Romans 8:18–25).

So we see that the evangelical faith—the biblical faith—is an essentially Trinitarian faith. We believe in God the Father, the God of creation, covenant, and revelation. We believe in God the Son, unique in his person, work, and salvation. And we believe in God the Holy Spirit, the Spirit of life, truth, holiness, love, and glory.

While our Christian creed is Trinitarian, it is also Christological—it focuses on Christ. For the Father sent the Son to be the Saviour of the world, and the Holy Spirit bears witness to him, Jesus, that he is Lord (1 John 4:14; 1 Corinthians 12:3). The major attacks on Christianity down the centuries have not surprisingly been attacks on the person and works of Christ. For this reason it has been vital for evangelical confessions of faith to articulate clearly their tenets of belief about him. It is for this reason also that Scripture's authority and justification by faith were the two major emphases of the Reformation, and are the two major hallmarks of evangelical Christians today.[21]

Why is this? It is because bound up with the finality of Jesus Christ, with what God has said and done in Christ definitively, evangelicals believe that God, who spoke in many ways and in many parts through 'the prophets to the fathers, spoke his final word in Christ and in the apostolic witness to Christ. Evangelicals also believe that God, who was active in mighty works throughout the history of Israel, performed his final deed in Christ crucified and risen. Jesus is both God's last word to the world and God's last saving deed for the world until he comes again. In other words, God's revelation and God's redemption were both finished in Christ; the adverb

21. See the *Westminster Confession of Faith*, completed in 1647, for the fullest exposition of evangelical belief following the Reformation. It opens with a finely crafted ten-clause section laying out the nature of Scripture; its supreme authority and sufficiency for all matters of belief and life.

hapax or *ephapax* (which means 'once and for all and for ever') is applied in the New Testament to both.

So if we start adding our words to the word that God has spoken in Christ, or if we start adding our works to the work that God has finished in Christ, we would be declaring Christ's word and work to be unsatisfactory, even incomplete. Nothing arouses evangelical indignation more than doctrines which undermine the complete satisfactoriness of what God has done and said in Christ. Nothing is more characteristic of evangelicals than a holy, even a vehement, jealousy for the unique glory of our Lord and Saviour Jesus Christ.

II. What Is Our Part, in Our Lifetime?

We come now to explore our personal responsibility to the evangelical faith, and what it means to keep it and to pass it on. For each generation has its own unique responsibility for that; in the family, in the church, and in teaching new Christians in every context. Let me suggest that we have four major duties, set out for us in Scripture.

Believe it and confess it

The evangelical faith is the gospel. It is the good news of salvation from God through Christ by the Holy Spirit. Our first responsibility, therefore, is to *embrace* it ourselves with all our hearts and minds secretly, and then go on to *confess* it with our lips publicly. For, as Paul wrote in Romans 10:9, 'If you confess with your lips that Jesus is Lord and believe in your heart that God has raised him from the dead you shall be saved.' Let me add a clarification. We must not separate belief in the evangelical faith from belief in Jesus, or putting our trust in Jesus. For in the New Testament they go together.

It is not possible to trust in Jesus without first defining who this Jesus is in whom we are putting our trust. Nor is it possible to believe the evangelical faith in our intellect and not trust personally in Jesus on whom our faith focuses. True faith is neither an arid assent to the evangelical faith with the mind alone; nor a mindless commitment to an undefined Jesus. Real faith is a conviction about the historic Jesus leading to a commitment to him today. It is our total commitment (mind, heart, will, and life) to the total Christ (who is God, man, Saviour, and Lord). So, let us not be ashamed to confess publicly that this is the Jesus in whom we believe and that our commitment to him is total. Our first responsibility to the evangelical faith is to believe and confess it.

Obey it and adorn it

In the New Testament, faith and obedience are inseparable twins. Linguistically it is significant that the passive of the verb *peitho*, meaning 'to be persuaded,' is sometimes translated 'to believe' (e.g. Acts 17:4; 26:28), and sometimes 'to obey' (e.g. Romans 2:8; Galatians 3:1). This is because when we are persuaded, we both believe and obey, and each is impossible without the other. Paul writes twice, at the beginning and end of Romans (1:5; 16:26) of 'the obedience of faith.' And in Hebrews 11 we read that 'by faith Abraham obeyed' (v. 8). It is inconceivable that we should trust Jesus without obeying him; or that we should commit ourselves to him as Saviour and withhold ourselves from him as Lord; or that we should believe the evangelical faith and it should have no effect upon our lives. No, everywhere in the New Testament God's truth is something to be done, not something only to be believed. It carries with it demands, duties, obligations. The evangelical faith radically transforms those who believe and embrace it.

Then, whenever we obey the gospel, we thereby adorn it. This expression comes in the letter to Titus (2:10), where Christian slaves in a domestic household are told to be honest, conscientious, submissive, and loyal 'so that in everything they may adorn the doctrine of God our Saviour.' Christian doctrine is salvation doctrine, and is adorned by those whose salvation is obvious in their behaviour. This verb 'to adorn' (*kosmeo*, from which we get our word cosmetic) is used in the New Testament of women adorned with clothing and jewels (1 Timothy 2:9), of a bride adorned for her husband (1 Peter 3:15; Revelation 21:2), and of the temple in Jerusalem adorned with noble stones (Luke 21:5). Adornment enhances the beauty of the person or of the building. Just so, a holy and Christlike life sets the gospel forth in its best light, displays its beauty and nobility, and makes it attractive to the beholder. There is an urgent need for us evangelical Christians to adorn the evangelical faith, or, as Paul put in Philippians 1:27, 'to live a life that is worthy of the gospel of Christ.' It's no use proclaiming the good news if people can't see it working itself out in your life.

Evangelical Christians, being gospel Christians, need (i) to live gospel lives—simple, consistent, Christlike; (ii) to build gospel homes, in which husband and wife love each other and their children, and in which the children love and honour their parents and are brought up in the discipline and instruction of the Lord Jesus; and (iii) develop gospel churches, whose worship is real, whose fellowship is caring, and whose outreach is compassionate.

How can we claim to believe the evangelical faith if we do not obey it? What is the point of confessing it with our lips if we do not adorn it in our lives, our homes, and our churches?

Proclaim it and argue it

The evangelical faith is not only to be believed, confessed, obeyed, and adorned; it is also to be actively spread. So every 'evangelical' (that is, somebody who believes the evangelical faith) should be an 'evangelist' (somebody who propagates it). For 'evangelism' means precisely to spread the 'evangel.'

But evangelism especially in our secularised society is not as easy as we have sometimes made out.

We tend to make one of two opposite mistakes. The first mistake is to recite biblical phrases, declaring that people need to be 'born again,' or 'saved,' or 'justified by faith,' or 'washed in the blood of the lamb,' or that they must 'enter the kingdom of God,' and people wonder what on earth we are talking about. The second and opposite mistake is to struggle so hard to translate the gospel into meaningful modern terms that the end product bears little resemblance to the New Testament. Both mistakes are made from excellent motives: to be faithful to Scripture, and to communicate intelligibly. We have to learn to do both simultaneously; to present the good news in terms that are equally loyal to Scripture and relevant to the contemporary world.

This principle holds good whoever the person is we are longing to win for Jesus. It might be a Marxist student in a British university, or an Arab Muslim or an Israeli Jew in the Middle East, or a Buddhist in Thailand, or a Hindu in India, or a scientific secularist, or a so-called 'Christian' whose allegiance to Jesus is purely nominal. In each case, there is a cultural barrier to overcome or a cultural chasm to bridge. In fact, there is a sense in which all authentic evangelism is cross-cultural. In it we are called to follow the model Jesus gave us in the incarnation. The incarnation is the most spectacular cross-cultural event in the history of the world. God's Son entered our world. He left the culture of heaven and he entered into the culture of the earth. We too have to learn to enter other people's worlds, both their thought world and the personal world of their pain, alienation, and loneliness. Only then, when we are inside their territory, which is home to them though alien to us, can we share with them the good news in a way that they will understand.

Such proclamation or witness will include argument—not the argument of heated debate, but the argument of 'reasoning with people out of the Scriptures.' We cannot proclaim the gospel to people in a dogmatic, take-it-or-leave-it style. We have to be sensitive to people's hang-ups and misunderstandings. We are called to be advocates as well as heralds. To be sure, no evangelism can ever be successful without the work of the Holy Spirit. He is the chief witness, the chief communicator, the chief evangelist. For he is the Spirit of truth, and without his illumination nobody can come to believe. Therefore Paul, for example, trusted entirely in what he called 'the demonstration of the Spirit and of power' (1 Corinthians 2:4); when he visited Thessalonica, the gospel did not come to them in word only but also 'in power and in the Holy Spirit' (1 Thessalonians 1:5). Nevertheless Paul also used arguments. Luke describes him in Thessalonica, Ephesus, Corinth, and elsewhere as 'arguing' with people out of the Scriptures, and 'persuading' them that Jesus was the Christ (e.g. Acts 17:2–4). It did not occur to Paul that argument and the Holy Spirit could be incompatible with one another. For it is through our explanations and our arguments that the Holy Spirit brings people to repentance and faith. So we have to proclaim and argue the evangelical faith, the gospel.

The gospel needs to be made known visually as well as verbally. People have to see as well as hear the good news. I am not now thinking of the way a holy life adorns the gospel, to which I have already referred, but rather of good works of compassion. Words and works went together in the public ministry of Jesus, the former proclaiming and the latter demonstrating the good news of the kingdom of God. So with us. This is the place for both philanthropy (works of mercy) and social action (the quest for justice). They manifest the love of God we preach. They are the good works by which, Jesus said, our light will shine and our heavenly Father be glorified (Matthew 5:16).

Defend it and suffer for it

Having given thanks for the Philippians' 'partnership in the gospel from the first day until now,' Paul describes them as sharing with him 'in the defence and confirmation of the gospel' (Philippians 1:7). He also describes himself as 'put here' (that is, in prison) 'for the defence of the gospel' (v16). Twice he uses the Greek word *apologia* (a defence), and once the word *bebaiosis* (a confirmation). Then at the end of the chapter, verse 27, he urges them to 'contend for the faith of the gospel,' to fight for it, because it is true. If we put all those phrases together our fight for the evangelical faith is to be both negative (defending it against attack) and positive (establishing or confirming its truth).

From the beginning the evangelical faith was 'spoken against.' The Jews in Rome used the expression about Paul and what they called the 'sect' or 'party' to which they understood he belonged. 'We know,' they said, 'that everywhere it is spoken against' (Acts 28:22). Jesus and his apostles gave the plainest possible warnings of false teachers who would arise, opposing the gospel. They called them 'wolves' who would infiltrate their way into God's flock, savaging, dividing, and even scattering the sheep. So 'Watch!' they said. 'Be on your guard! Keep alert!' Pastors in particular have to be loyal to apostolic teaching, so that we can encourage people by sound doctrine and refute those who oppose it (Titus 1:9).

Attacks against the Christian faith will always change with the times. As well as those who declare that Jesus was no more than a good man, or that all religions lead to God, we now have the rise of Islam in political and religious terms, as well as all the avenues into which postmodernity has led us: the New Atheism in its diverse forms, particularly in the West and in academia; a sense that anything is possible for mankind to achieve with sophisticated advances in technology; a widespread confounding of the biblical view of sexuality; and insidiously, a denial that words carry an intended meaning. We could go on.

Over against such threats, we are called to defend the faith, and to be ready at all times to 'give an answer' (*apologia*, again a defence) 'to everyone who asks us the reason for the hope' that is in us (1 Peter 3:15). So we have to read and think and discuss. Further, we must pray that God will raise up more gifted apologists, who will out-think the opponents of the Christian faith, and re-establish it as the faith of the church.

Some evangelicals seem to want all their fellow Christians to dot every 'i' and cross every 't' of their own particular belief. This is neither wise nor possible this side of heaven. So 'within the family,' among those who are committed to Christ and seemingly anxious to understand and follow the Bible, we must allow one another a certain liberty of interpretation, e.g. over the precise volume of water that is necessary to validate a baptism, or which spiritual gifts are more important than others, or how prophecy is to be applied today, etc. These are family discussions, debates within the family.

But when some fundamental of the evangelical faith is under attack, we cannot remain indifferent or silent. The apostle John called 'antichrist' those teachers who denied the divine-human person of Jesus (1 John 2:18–25). The apostle Paul called down God's judgment on any teacher who contradicted the gospel of his free grace in Christ (Galatians 1:6–9). The apostle Paul opposed the apostle Peter in public when Peter, by his actions, denied the truth of the gospel (Galatians 1:11–16). Very painful and embarrassing confrontations are sometimes necessary today if a vital doctrine is at stake.

We cannot defend the gospel without suffering for it, but we should never court opposition. Yet we must be ready to suffer for the evangelical faith in which we believe. For 'it has been given to

us,' Paul wrote in Philippians 1:29, 'not only to believe in Christ but also to suffer for his sake.' Many
of our brothers and sisters are suffering physical
persecution for their faithfulness in the world today.
Fanatical opponents of the gospel, whether Hindu
or Muslim or Marxist, are beating them up, burning churches, confiscating Bibles, putting them in
prison or labour camps, even liquidating them. We
in the West are less likely to suffer physical attack
than ridicule and social ostracism for the name of
Jesus. That can be very painful too. But since Jesus
did not hesitate to endure for us the shame and pain
of the cross, we should not be surprised (if we are
called upon to suffer), as though some strange thing
were happening to us. Still less should we wallow
in self-pity. We should rejoice that we are given the
privilege of sharing in the sufferings of Christ (Acts
5:41; 1 Peter 4:12–14).

To conclude, we have seen that the evangelical
faith is neither more nor less than the historic Christian faith. It is the Trinitarian faith, in all its balanced
fulness. It is the original, biblical, apostolic faith
about God the Father, the Son, and the Holy Spirit.

We have also seen that our responsibility is to
believe and confess it, to obey and adorn it, to proclaim and argue it, and to defend and (if necessary)
suffer for it.

May God give us wisdom and courage in these
diverse ways to keep the faith in our own generation,
preserved for us so wonderfully by the Reformers,
and to pass it on.

APPENDICES

Jesus' Prayer for Unity in His Church

Alan Purser

John 17 is holy ground: Jesus prays for unity, that his church may be one. For this is the key to effective mission. It is a passage which has often been misunderstood.

I recall hearing a church leader say that the most serious cause of failure to evangelize our country was disunity within Christ's church. Referring to Jesus' prayer recorded in John 17, he pointed to Christ's ardent desire for unity amongst his disciples, and the close connection between such unity and effective mission (17:21).

Alan Purser has served in parish ministry in the UK, in student ministry in South Africa, and on the staff of the Proclamation Trust and BCMS Crosslinks. Travelling widely in Africa and Europe, he has worked to promote a biblical theology of mission, and to root today's practice of mission engagement in the instruction of Jesus and his apostles.

This raises the question of what exactly Jesus was saying, and leads us back to the text to investigate. In John 17 it is obvious how important unity is—three times Jesus prays for it (vv. 21, 22, 23)—so we are bound to ask 'Who is such unity to be between?' and 'What kind of unity is meant?' 'What could be the connection between unity and effective mission'?

In a series of expositions from what we know as the Upper Room Discourse, delivered to the North American student missions convention in Urbana, John Stott brought a note of caution. These prayers, so often quoted, had, he said, come to be the proof texts of the ecumenical movement. It was important to understand their context if we are to interpret them correctly, and not be unbalanced, or even mistaken, in their interpretation. He went on to urge 'careful and critical scrutiny.'[22]

Here we attempt to give them that scrutiny, for a study of these words offers far-reaching implications for church and mission today.

The structure of Jesus' prayer is straightforward—first he prays for himself (see vv. 1–5), then for the disciples (vv. 6–19) and finally for 'those who will believe through their testimony' (vv. 20–26). The content of each phrase, however, varies. Now that Jesus' hour has finally come, his prayer for himself is that he might be glorified in carrying out his Father's will, with all the suffering that will entail. Turning to pray for the disciples, Jesus asks that they might be

22. John Stott's addresses (1964). See urbana.org for its growing video archive.

sanctified (set apart) *for*, and *by*, the truth—the truth
that is found in God's word—for this is how they
will be able to withstand the enmity of the world. It
was to this group of eleven soon-to-be apostles, that
Jesus had already made promises about the gift of the
Holy Spirit. For the Holy Sprit would enable them
to recall all that he had taught them, and lead them
into all that truth which they were not yet able to embrace (see 14:26; 16:8–11). Although Jesus prays that
the apostles may be '*one, even as we are one*' (v. 11) it
is not until the third phase of his prayer that his peti-
tions focus chiefly on unity. So let us look at 17:20–26
in greater detail.

'*I do not ask for these only, but also for those who
will believe in me through their word*' (v. 20). As Stott
pointed out to the students, 'Here Christ distin-
guishes between the apostles for whom he has just
been praying and those who would later believe in
him through their teaching.' This distinction is vital
if we are to make sense of what follows. Stott empha-
sizes the point:

'Jesus alludes to two groups, conveniently des-
ignated "*these*" (i.e. the apostles) and "*those*"' (i.e.
subsequent believers). It seems beyond question that
the "*all*" of verse 21, whose unity Christ desires, are a
combination of "*these*" and "*those*." Let me elaborate
on this. The Lord Jesus peers with prophetic eyes into
the future. He sees generation after generation of his
followers. He calls them "*believers*," for they will believe in him, and they will believe in him through the
apostles' words. This is a description of every single

Christian believer from the Day of Pentecost onward, including ourselves . . . here then are the two groups—the little band of chosen apostles ("*these*") and the huge company who will believe in Jesus through their word ("*those*"). And Christ's prayer is that "*all*" (both "*these*" and "*those*") may be one.'

Let's pause a moment, and not miss this. Jesus is first and foremost asking his Father for unity between the apostolic church of the first century and the church of subsequent centuries. He is praying that we might believe the same truths, follow the same Lord, proclaim the same message, obey the same teaching, suffer for the same cause, and share in the same hope. This is in accord with the description of the first converts who, Luke tells us, '*devoted themselves to the apostles' teaching and fellowship*' (Acts 2:42). As a result of the fulfillment of Jesus' promises to them the New Testament was written, which makes it possible for every subsequent generation to devote themselves similarly to the teaching of the apostles. Here then is the kind of apostolic succession envisaged by Jesus. This is the unity for which he prayed.

A further aspect of that unity is articulated in the second half of verse 21, '*that they also may be in us.*' Jesus' eternal fellowship with the Father shows the pattern for the relationship between the church and the Godhead. It speaks of an organic unity. Again Stott put it helpfully, 'The unity of the church for which Christ prayed was not primarily that we may be one with each other, but first that we may be one with the apostles, and second that we may be one with the Father and the Son. The first speaks of a common truth, the second of a common life. And both are needed to unite the church.'

So the means of establishing and maintaining unity is common truth. Far from the popular notion that doctrine divides, Jesus taught the opposite—unity amongst the apostles would be secured by their loyalty to the divine revelation (v. 11), and unity in the later church would be secured in the same way. Stott insists, 'It is not by neglecting Christ or the apostolic witness to Christ that the church's unity will be secured. Rather the reverse. The unity of the church is unity in the truth. To quote Hugh Latimer: "Unity must be according to God's holy word, or else it were better war than peace. We ought never to regard unity so much that we forsake God's word for her sake." '[23]

What then of the connection between unity and mission? In all that Jesus prays, the purpose of this kind of unity is missiological, *so that the world may believe* (vv. 21, 23). They will always be closely linked as evangelism is central to the calling of the whole church. Indeed it is the very object and purpose of this unity. So we must all work to maintain this unity until the ultimate goal of heaven is reached (v. 24).

We conclude with John Stott's summary: 'So truth, holiness, unity and mission belong together and cannot be separated.'

---

23. Latimer's second sermon preached in the county of Lincolnshire (*Sermons*, 1:487).

Martin Luther's 95 Theses

Out of love for the truth and the desire to bring it to light, the following propositions will be discussed at Wittenberg, under the presidency of the Reverend Father Martin Luther, Master of Arts and of Sacred Theology, and Lecturer in Ordinary on the same at that place. Wherefore he requests that those who are unable to be present and debate orally with us, may do so by letter.

In the Name our Lord Jesus Christ. Amen.

1. Our Lord and Master Jesus Christ, when He said *Poenitentiam agite*, willed that the whole life of believers should be repentance.

2. This word cannot be understood to mean sacramental penance, i.e. confession and satisfaction, which is administered by the priests.

3. Yet it means not inward repentance only; nay, there is no inward repentance which does not outwardly work divers mortifications of the flesh.

4. The penalty [of sin], therefore, continues so long as hatred of self continues; for this is the true inward repentance, and continues until our entrance into the kingdom of heaven.

5. The pope does not intend to remit, and cannot remit any penalties other than those which he has imposed either by his own authority or by that of the canons.

6. The pope cannot remit any guilt, except by declaring that it has been remitted by God and by assenting to God's remission; though, to be sure, he may grant remission in cases reserved to his judgment. If his right to grant remission in such cases were despised, the guilt would remain entirely unforgiven.

7. God remits guilt to no one whom He does not, at the same time, humble in all things and bring into subjection to His vicar, the priest.

8. The penitential canons are imposed only on the living, and, according to them, nothing should be imposed on the dying.

9. Therefore the Holy Spirit in the pope is kind to us, because in his decrees he always makes exception of the article of death and of necessity.

10. Ignorant and wicked are the doings of those priests who, in the case of the dying, reserve canonical penances for purgatory.

11. This changing of the canonical penalty to the penalty of purgatory is quite evidently one of the tares that were sown while the bishops slept.

12. In former times the canonical penalties were imposed not after, but before absolution, as tests of true contrition.

13. The dying are freed by death from all penalties; they are already dead to canonical rules, and have a right to be released from them.

14. The imperfect health [of soul], that is to say, the imperfect love, of the dying brings with it, of necessity, great fear; and the smaller the love, the greater is the fear.

15. This fear and horror is sufficient of itself alone (to say nothing of other things) to constitute the penalty of purgatory, since it is very near to the horror of despair.

16. Hell, purgatory, and heaven seem to differ as do despair, almost-despair, and the assurance of safety.

17. With souls in purgatory it seems necessary that horror should grow less and love increase.

18. It seems unproved, either by reason or Scripture, that they are outside the state of merit, that is to say, of increasing love.

19. Again, it seems unproved that they, or at least that all of them, are certain or assured of their own blessedness, though we may be quite certain of it.

20. Therefore by 'full remission of all penalties' the pope means not actually 'of all,' but only of those imposed by himself.

21. Therefore those preachers of indulgences are in error, who say that by the pope's indulgences a man is freed from every penalty, and sjaved;

22. Whereas he remits to souls in purgatory no penalty which, according to the canons, they would have had to pay in this life.

23. If it is at all possible to grant to any one the remission of all penalties whatsoever, it is certain that this remission can be granted only to the most perfect, that is, to the very fewest.

24. It must needs be, therefore, that the greater part of the people are deceived by that indiscriminate and high-sounding promise of release from penalty.

25. The power which the pope has, in a general way, over purgatory, is just like the power which any bishop or curate has, in a special way, within his own diocese or parish.

26. The pope does well when he grants remission to souls [in purgatory], not by the power of the keys (which he does not possess), but by way of intercession.

27. They preach man who say that so soon as the penny jingles into the money-box, the soul flies out [of purgatory].

28. It is certain that when the penny jingles into the money-box, gain and avarice can be increased, but the result of the intercession of the Church is in the power of God alone.

29. Who knows whether all the souls in purgatory wish to be bought out of it, as in the legend of Sts. Severinus and Paschal.

30. No one is sure that his own contrition is sincere; much less that he has attained full remission.

31. Rare as is the man that is truly penitent, so rare is also the man who truly buys indulgences, i.e. such men are most rare.

32. They will be condemned eternally, together with their teachers, who believe themselves

sure of their salvation because they have letters of pardon.

33. Men must be on their guard against those who say that the pope's pardons are that inestimable gift of God by which man is reconciled to Him;

34. For these 'graces of pardon' concern only the penalties of sacramental satisfaction, and these are appointed by man.

35. They preach no Christian doctrine who teach that contrition is not necessary in those who intend to buy souls out of purgatory or to buy confessionalia.

36. Every truly repentant Christian has a right to full remission of penalty and guilt, even without letters of pardon.

37. Every true Christian, whether living or dead, has part in all the blessings of Christ and the Church; and this is granted him by God, even without letters of pardon.

38. Nevertheless, the remission and participation [in the blessings of the Church] which are granted by the pope are in no way to be despised, for they are, as I have said, the declaration of divine remission.

39. It is most difficult, even for the very keenest theologians, at one and the same time to commend to the people the abundance of pardons and [the need of] true contrition.

40. True contrition seeks and loves penalties, but liberal pardons only relax penalties and cause them to be hated, or at least, furnish an occasion [for hating them].

41. Apostolic pardons are to be preached with caution, lest the people may falsely think them preferable to other good works of love.

42. Christians are to be taught that the pope does not intend the buying of pardons to be compared in any way to works of mercy.

43. Christians are to be taught that he who gives to the poor or lends to the needy does a better work than buying pardons;

44. Because love grows by works of love, and man becomes better; but by pardons man does not grow better, only more free from penalty.

45. Christians are to be taught that he who sees a man in need, and passes him by, and gives [his money] for pardons, purchases not the indulgences of the pope, but the indignation of God.

46. Christians are to be taught that unless they have more than they need, they are bound to keep back what is necessary for their own families, and by no means to squander it on pardons.

47. Christians are to be taught that the buying of pardons is a matter of free will, and not of commandment.

48. Christians are to be taught that the pope, in granting pardons, needs, and therefore desires, their devout prayer for him more than the money they bring.

49. Christians are to be taught that the pope's pardons are useful, if they do not put their trust in them; but altogether harmful, if through them they lose their fear of God.

50. Christians are to be taught that if the pope knew the exactions of the pardon-preachers, he would rather that St. Peter's church should go to ashes, than that it should be built up with the skin, flesh, and bones of his sheep.

51. Christians are to be taught that it would be the pope's wish, as it is his duty, to give of his own money to very many of those from whom certain hawkers of pardons cajole money, even though the church of St. Peter might have to be sold.

52. The assurance of salvation by letters of pardon is vain, even though the commissary, nay, even though the pope himself, were to stake his soul upon it.

53. They are enemies of Christ and of the pope, who bid the Word of God be altogether silent in some Churches, in order that pardons may be preached in others.

54. Injury is done the Word of God when, in the same sermon, an equal or a longer time is spent on pardons than on this Word.

55. It must be the intention of the pope that if pardons, which are a very small thing, are celebrated with one bell, with single processions and ceremonies, then the Gospel, which is the very greatest thing, should be preached with a hundred bells, a hundred processions, a hundred ceremonies.

56. The 'treasures of the Church,' out of which the pope grants indulgences, are not sufficiently named or known among the people of Christ.

57. That they are not temporal treasures is certainly evident, for many of the vendors do not pour out such treasures so easily, but only gather them.

58. Nor are they the merits of Christ and the Saints, for even without the pope, these always work grace for the inner man, and the cross, death, and hell for the outward man.

59. Saint Lawrence said that the treasures of the Church were the Church's poor, but he spoke according to the usage of the word in his own time.

60. Without rashness we say that the keys of the Church, given by Christ's merit, are that treasure;

61. For it is clear that for the remission of penalties and of reserved cases, the power of the pope is of itself sufficient.

62. The true treasure of the Church is the Most Holy Gospel of the glory and the grace of God.

63. But this treasure is naturally most odious, for it makes the first to be last.

64. On the other hand, the treasure of indulgences is naturally most acceptable, for it makes the last to be first.

65. Therefore the treasures of the Gospel are nets with which they formerly were wont to fish for men of riches.

66. The treasures of the indulgences are nets with which they now fish for the riches of men.

67. The indulgences which the preachers cry as the 'greatest graces' are known to be truly such, in so far as they promote gain.

68. Yet they are in truth the very smallest graces compared with the grace of God and the piety of the Cross.

69. Bishops and curates are bound to admit the commissaries of apostolic pardons, with all reverence.

70. But still more are they bound to strain all their eyes and attend with all their ears, lest these men preach their own dreams instead of the commission of the pope.

71. He who speaks against the truth of apostolic pardons, let him be anathema and accursed!

72. But he who guards against the lust and license of the pardon-preachers, let him be blessed!

73. The pope justly thunders against those who, by any art, contrive the injury of the traffic in pardons.

74. But much more does he intend to thunder against those who use the pretext of pardons to contrive the injury of holy love and truth.

75. To think the papal pardons so great that they could absolve a man even if he had committed an impossible sin and violated the Mother of God—this is madness.

76. We say, on the contrary, that the papal pardons are not able to remove the very least of venial sins, so far as its guilt is concerned.

77. It is said that even St. Peter, if he were now Pope, could not bestow greater graces; this is blasphemy against St. Peter and against the pope.

78. We say, on the contrary, that even the present pope, and any pope at all, has greater graces at his disposal; to wit, the Gospel, powers, gifts of healing, etc., as it is written in 1 Corinthians 12.

79. To say that the cross, emblazoned with the papal arms, which is set up [by the preachers of indulgences], is of equal worth with the Cross of Christ, is blasphemy.

80. The bishops, curates, and theologians who allow such talk to be spread among the people, will have an account to render.

81. This unbridled preaching of pardons makes it no easy matter, even for learned men, to rescue the reverence due to the pope from

slander, or even from the shrewd questionings of the laity.

82. To wit:—'Why does not the pope empty purgatory, for the sake of holy love and of the dire need of the souls that are there, if he redeems an infinite number of souls for the sake of miserable money with which to build a Church? The former reasons would be most just; the latter is most trivial.'

83. Again:—'Why are mortuary and anniversary masses for the dead continued, and why does he not return or permit the withdrawal of the endowments founded on their behalf, since it is wrong to pray for the redeemed?'

84. Again:—'What is this new piety of God and the pope, that for money they allow a man who is impious and their enemy to buy out of purgatory the pious soul of a friend of God, and do not rather, because of that pious and beloved soul's own need, free it for pure love's sake?'

85. Again:—'Why are the penitential canons long since in actual fact and through disuse abrogated and dead, now satisfied by the granting of indulgences, as though they were still alive and in force?'

86. Again:—'Why does not the pope, whose wealth is today greater than the riches of the richest, build just this one church of St. Peter with his own money, rather than with the money of poor believers?'

87. Again:—'What is it that the pope remits, and what participation does he grant to those who, by perfect contrition, have a right to full remission and participation?'

88. Again:—'What greater blessing could come to the Church than if the pope were to do a hundred times a day what he now does once, and bestow on every believer these remissions and participations?'

89. 'Since the pope, by his pardons, seeks the salvation of souls rather than money, why does he suspend the indulgences and pardons granted heretofore, since these have equal efficacy?'

90. To repress these arguments and scruples of the laity by force alone, and not to resolve them by giving reasons, is to expose the Church and the pope to the ridicule of their enemies, and to make Christians unhappy.

91. If, therefore, pardons were preached according to the spirit and mind of the pope, all

these doubts would be readily resolved; nay, they would not exist.

92. Away, then, with all those prophets who say to the people of Christ, 'Peace, peace,' and there is no peace!

93. Blessed be all those prophets who say to the people of Christ, 'Cross, cross,' and there is no cross!

94. Christians are to be exhorted that they be diligent in following Christ, their Head, through penalties, deaths, and hell;

95. And thus be confident of entering into heaven rather through many tribulations, than through the assurance of peace.

Questions for Study
and Reflection

1. Consider four questions:

What are the doctrinal challenges to the evangelical faith in your context?

What are the cultural challenges for evangelicals in public life or the workplace?

How well are we passing on the baton of apostolic truth to the next generation? What can we do differently to achieve this better?

Could churches work together more fruitfully at a local level in some areas? Are there any activities in which it could stir confusion to work together?

2. Gain an overview of the Reformation

Read *The Unquenchable Flame* by Michael Reeves (IVP, 2009) or *Why the Reformation Still Matters* by Michael Reeves and Tim Chester (IVP, 2016).

OR

Listen-in to a class taught by Carl Trueman (Westminster Theological Seminary, Philadelphia). Thirty-three sessions available by podcast at www. wts.ac.

For those wanting to read further, we commend Andrew Pettegree's (ed) *The Reformation World* (Routledge, 2000). An in-depth, one-volume survey of the Reformation, well-illustrated.

3. Study a Confession of Faith

Read through *The Westminster Confession of Faith* (1647).

Recommended guide: *Confessing the Faith: A reader's guide to the Westminster Confession of Faith* by Chad Van Dixhoorn (Banner of Truth, 2016).

OR

Read through the *Cape Town Confession of Faith* (2010).

Recommended guide: *Cape Town Commitment Study Edition* by Rose Dowsett (Hendrickson Publishers / Lausanne Library, 2012).

4. Pray for the worldwide Church

Read the responses from Christian leaders in other regions (lausanne.org/reformation). What lessons can we draw for ourselves from the Church in these regions?

Recommended book: *Pray for the World* by Jason Mandryk and Molly Wall (IVP).

How can we better echo Christ's prayer for future generations?

5. Learn about Church history in your context

Read a book outlining the history of the evangelical church in your country. Who were its pioneers? What challenges has it faced internally, and from external pressures? Are there lessons other nations can learn from the challenges your church has faced?

Read the story of a church from another part of the world which has come through a particular trial in standing for truth.

6. Discuss the task of the Church now

Select one or two books for the group to read and discuss, relating to specialist areas, or to the need more generally for a Christian voice. For example:

The Courage to be Protestant by David F Wells (Eerdmans 2008).

Impossible People by Os Guinness (IVP).

Fruitfulness on the Frontline by Mark Greene (IVP).

Recommended Reading

From the Lausanne Movement

The Lausanne Legacy: Landmarks in Global Mission. Edited by J E M Cameron (Hendrickson Publishers).

The Cape Town Commitment: A Call to Action. A Study Guide for Small Groups. Compiled by Sara Singleton and Matt Ristuccia (Hendrickson Publishers).

The Cape Town Commitment: Study Edition by Rose Dowsett (Hendrickson Publishers).

Ephesians: Studying with the Global Church by Lindsay Olesberg. Six-week study guide for home groups (Hendrickson Publishers).

Creation Care and the Gospel. Edited by Colin Bell and Robert S White (Hendrickson Publishers).

The Glory of the Cross by James Philip (Hendrickson Publishers).

The Grace of Giving: Money and the Gospel by John Stott and Christ Wright (Hendrickson Publishers).

Lausanne Movement

Connecting influencers and ideas for global mission

The Lausanne Movement takes its name from the International Congress on World Evangelization, convened in 1974 in Lausanne, Switzerland, by the US evangelist Billy Graham. His long-time friend John Stott, the UK pastor-theologian, was chief architect of *The Lausanne Covenant*, which issued from this gathering.

Two further global Congresses followed—the second in Manila, Philippines (1989) and the third in Cape Town, South Africa (2010). From the Third Lausanne Congress came *The Cape Town Commitment: A Confession of Faith and a Call to Action*. Its Call to Action was the fruit of a careful process conducted over four years to discern what we believe the Holy Spirit is saying to the global church in our times. In the words of the *Commitment*'s chief architect, Chris Wright, it expresses 'the conviction of a Movement and the voice of a multitude.'

The Lausanne Movement connects evangelical influencers across regions and across generations: in the church, in ministries, and in the workplace.

Under God, Lausanne events have often acted as a powerful catalyst; as a result, strategic ideas such as Unreached People Groups, the 10/40 Window, and holistic/integral mission have been introduced to missional thinking. Over 30 specialist Issue Networks now focus on the outworking of the priorities outlined in *The Cape Town Commitment*.

The movement makes available online over 40 years of missional content. Sign up to receive *Lausanne Global Analysis* to your inbox. Watch videos from Lausanne's gatherings. On the website you will also find a complete list of titles in the Lausanne Library.

www.lausanne.org